HUNTING: *PURSUING WILD GAME!* ™

WING SHOOTING

JENNIFER BRINGLE

rosen publishing's
rosen central

New York

To my uncle Jerry and all the other hunters and fishermen in my family

Published in 2011 by The Rosen Publishing Group, Inc.
29 East 21st Street, New York, NY 10010

First Edition

Library of Congress Cataloging-in-Publication Data

Bringle, Jennifer.
Wing shooting / Jennifer Bringle. — 1st ed.
    p. cm. — (Hunting: pursuing wild game!)
Includes bibliographical references and index.
ISBN 978-1-4488-1241-7 (library binding) —
ISBN 978-1-4488-2271-3 (pbk.) —
ISBN 978-1-4488-2280-5 (6-pack)
1. Fowling—Juvenile literature. I. Title.
SK315.B75 2011
799.2'4—dc22

                                                                    2010018465

Manufactured in Malaysia

CPSIA Compliance Information: Batch #W11YA: For further information, contact Rosen Publishing, New York, New York, at 1-800-237-9932.

On the cover: A pheasant hides from hunters and looks for food in the tall prairie grasses.

CONTENTS

INTRODUCTION 4

CHAPTER 1 7
HUNTER EDUCATION

CHAPTER 2 17
HUNTER RESPONSIBILITY

CHAPTER 3 24
PLANNING THE HUNT

CHAPTER 4 36
HUNTING

CHAPTER 5 48
AFTER THE HUNT

GLOSSARY 55

FOR MORE INFORMATION 57

FOR FURTHER READING 59

BIBLIOGRAPHY 60

INDEX 62

*H*unting is one of the most popular pastimes in the United States and Canada. Millions of people go hunting each year, and hunters sometimes travel great distances to pursue their sport. They use guns, archery equipment, and sometimes dogs to help them find and harvest animals.

But hunting is not a new thing. For thousands of years, people have hunted animals. In centuries past, people hunted to feed themselves and their families. They used the animal furs and skins to make clothing and shelter. In modern times, hunting has evolved into more of a sport than a necessity, but it remains just as popular.

Hunters capture and harvest animals for sport, but also for other reasons. Although they don't have to, some hunters still hunt for food. Often, the game they hunt, such as birds and deer, provides meat not available in most stores. People also sometimes hunt to eliminate pests that endanger crops or other animals. Hunters can also help regulate animal populations, preventing overpopulation in areas where there aren't natural predators to do it.

But hunters must be careful, and they must be certain to hunt legally. Conservation laws are set in place

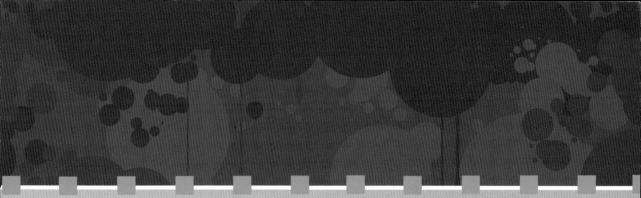

to protect animal populations from overhunting. These laws set legal hunting areas, and hunting seasons, to ensure that a normal population size of animals is maintained. It is up to hunters to be aware of these designated areas and times in order to hunt responsibly and ethically.

Hunters must be certain to have the proper licenses and permits, as well as knowledge of legal hunting seasons and approved areas, before heading out on a hunt.

Hunters must also be certain to get the proper licenses and permits to hunt in their state. Different states have different rules and licensing requirements, and it's up to the hunters to be aware of those rules and regulations. They must be certain to have the proper licenses and permits before they go hunting.

Part of the licensing process includes taking hunter safety courses. It's very important for hunters to take these classes to learn the proper procedures for hunts and to learn gun and weapon safety. These classes teach hunters the things they need to know to keep themselves, and other hunters, safe during hunting trips.

Of the many different types of hunting, wing shooting is one of the most popular. Wing shooting is shooting game birds in flight. Wing shooting is also sometimes called upland hunting, as the birds being hunted are called upland birds. This type of hunting is difficult because the target is moving, often at high speeds, through midair. Game birds hunted in wing shooting are usually small birds such as doves, pheasants, grouse, chukar (also called chukar partridge), and prairie chickens. Hunters use shotguns and sometimes archery equipment and dogs to hunt these birds.

Before wing shooting, hunters must be knowledgeable about both their hunting targets and the practice of hunting itself. They must be ready to hunt legally, ethically, and most importantly, safely.

CHAPTER 1

HUNTER EDUCATION

No matter what type of game a hunter is hunting, he or she needs the proper weapon and equipment. Depending on the type of game, weapons used vary. For wing shooting, the most commonly used weapon is the shotgun. The kinds of shotguns used for wing shooting are over/unders, semiautomatics, and the upland shotgun.

The double barrel over/under has two barrels stacked on top of each other, instead of side by side. A semiautomatic automatically loads; instead of having the action manually operated by a pump or lever, the action automatically cycles each time the shotgun is fired, ejecting the spent shell and reloading a fresh one into the chamber. The upland shotgun has side-by-side double barrels that are shorter than the average shotgun. Shorter barrels allow fast movement and easy maneuverability,

Before going on a hunt, wing shooters must learn proper safety procedures and gun techniques. It's important to know all about the gun and how to safely use it.

which is essential for shooting fast-moving birds.

Wing shooters also often opt for lighter-weight guns. This is because wing shooters have to do quite a bit of walking when looking for the right hunting area. The downside of having a lighter shotgun is that a lighter gun is harder to control than a heavier one. With a lighter gun, the gun's swing momentum can cause the gun to get out of control. Hunters using lighter weight guns must have strong body strength and control in order to keep a handle on their guns.

There are several different shotgun gauges. Common shotgun gauges are 10 gauge, 12 gauge, 16 gauge, 20 gauge, and 28 gauge. The smaller the gauge number, the larger the shotgun bore, or opening in the barrel. Gauge is determined by the number of lead balls of size equal to the approximate diameter of the bore that it takes to weigh 1 pound (.45 kilogram). For example, it would take 12 lead balls with the same diameter as a 12-gauge shotgun bore to weigh one pound. The .410-bore shotgun is the only exception to the gauge designation for shotguns. It has an actual bore diameter of 410/1000ths

of an inch, which is approximately equivalent to a 67½ gauge.

Each gauge of shotgun shoots only shells of the same gauge. For example, 12-gauge guns use only 12-gauge shells. The gauge of a shotgun is usually marked on the rear of the barrel, and the gauge of a shell is marked on the shell as well as on the factory box.

When handling guns there are several important safety rules to remember:

- Always point the muzzle of a firearm or a bow and arrow in a safe direction. Never point it toward yourself or another hunter.
- Treat every firearm or bow with the same respect you would show a loaded gun or nocked arrow. Even if a hunter thinks a gun or bow is unloaded, he or she still needs to be very careful.
- Be sure of the target and what is in front of and behind the target.
- Unload and safely store firearms or unstring conventional bows when not in use.
- Handle firearms, arrows, and ammunition carefully. They are weapons that can cause serious injury or death and should be handled with extreme caution.

Following gun safety rules is an essential part of any hunt. In addition to properly handling and pointing the gun, shooters should use ear and eye protection to prevent injury or hearing loss.

- Know your safe zone of fire and stay in it. Stepping out of a safe shooting zone can put the hunter, as well as other hunters, in danger of accidents.

Hunter education courses are a requirement in most states and provinces. They usually cover hunting safety, firearms, bows, wildlife identification, wildlife management, survival, game care, ethics, responsibility, and regulations.

- Wear hearing and eye protection when shooting. Guns can be very loud, and since it's so close to the body, the volume of the gun can cause hearing loss. Guns can also sometimes fly back toward a hunter, or shells being expelled from the gun can fly into a hunter's face, so it's important to make sure the eyes are protected with hunting glasses.

Hunter Education

One of the most important aspects of hunting is education. Just as drivers must take driver education courses, hunters must take hunting education courses before they are able to obtain a hunting license. Hunter education is incredibly important, as it teaches hunters how to hunt safely, ethically, and legally.

Each state and Canadian province offers hunter education courses. Mandatory requirements differ by state or province. But, in general, most hunter education courses are taught according to standards established by the International Hunter Education Association (IHEA). These courses cover hunting safety, firearms, bows, wildlife identification, wildlife management, survival, game care, ethics, responsibility, and regulations.

The Importance of Hunter Safety

In 2002, a young man hunting near Shelbyville, Texas, was having a remarkable hunting day. It was late afternoon when a deer walked out of the brush, right into his gun's range. He shot and bagged the deer, thinking how lucky he'd been. Just at that time, a large buck stepped out right into his range again. Having bagged two deer, he couldn't believe his luck when he noticed movement in the brush again. It was nearly evening, but he decided to shoot one more time. He hit his mark, but instead of collecting another deer, he realized he'd made a horrible, tragic error—he accidentally shot a fellow hunter.

Knowing proper hunter safety procedures can mean the difference between life and death. Each year, hunters die or are injured unnecessarily because of the lack of good hunter safety practices.

In the Shelbyville case, both hunters made big mistakes that led to tragedy. The shooter shot before getting a good eye on his quarry, making it virtually impossible for him to identify his target. Since it was almost dark, this was even more important. He relied totally on sight, not bothering to listen for sound cues or check for behavioral or movement cues. And the victim neglected to wear enough hunter orange to stand out from the brush. Had he worn the proper orange attire, he might have been recognized as a person, rather than a deer.

Hunters must always put safety first when on the hunt. Knowing the proper safety procedures, and always following them, is essential for a safe, enjoyable hunt.

Hunting safety is one of the most important aspects of hunter education courses. Some basic hunting safety tips to remember include:

- Tell someone where you will be hunting. If you get injured or lost, someone should be aware of your location.
- Avoid hunting alone. If you must go alone, hunt in familiar areas.
- Dress properly. If it's cold, be sure to dress warmly enough to prevent hypothermia. If it's hot, be sure to wear lightweight clothing that will help prevent overheating. In sunny weather, sunscreen is a must, since hunters spend long hours outside in the sun. A hat and protective eyewear are also good additions to a hunter's wardrobe.
- Check hunting equipment before every hunting outing. Make sure each gun or other piece of equipment works properly and that you are familiar with the proper way to use it.
- Never carry a loaded weapon in a car or other vehicle. Be sure to unload guns when the hunt is finished.
- Wear enough hunter orange to make yourself visible to other hunters. A hunter orange hat or vest are both good items to help make hunters stand out against the landscape. Wearing hunter orange is required on public hunting areas.
- Be certain to hunt in designated hunting areas, and be mindful of the hunters around you. Make them aware of your presence to prevent accidents.
- Never drink or use drugs when hunting. Even if it's something as simple as cold medicine or cough syrup that could make you drowsy, you should never take it before hunting.
- Identify your target before shooting. Many hunting accidents and fatalities occur when hunters shoot before verifying their target. Use visual cues, listen for the bird's distinctive call, and

look for flight patterns to verify that what you're aiming at is a bird. Identification also helps prevent accidentally shooting birds that aren't supposed to be hunted.

Traditional hunter education courses usually require attendance at multiple instructor-led sessions. Students must pass written and/or skills tests to pass the course. Some states offer alternative class formats for those whose schedules don't allow them to attend a traditional class. These alternative classes include at-home study through online classes, written manuals, CDs, DVDs, or videotapes. But students in this type of course are still often required to attend some classes.

Generally, passing a hunter education course in one state or province will allow you to hunt in other states as well. Classes can be found either through state departments of natural resources or through the IHEA's Web site.

CHAPTER 2

HUNTER RESPONSIBILITY

*A*s a hunter, it's extremely important to follow the rules and regulations of the sport. These guidelines are set for a reason, and breaking them can endanger you and your fellow hunters. It can also disrupt vital ecosystems that make hunting possible in the first place.

Following Hunting Laws and Regulations

Just as drivers must get a license before hitting the road, most states require hunters to receive a hunting license or permit before going on a hunt. The specific qualifications and regulations for these licenses and permits vary from state to state, but in general, a person must meet the following requirements before receiving a hunting license or permit:

In order to hunt legally, wing shooters must obtain a hunting license or permit before going on a hunt. Different states and provinces have different requirements for these licenses and permits.

• Minimum age requirement: many states require that hunters reach a certain age before they are able to receive a license or permit.

• Residency requirement: most states require proof of residence in order to obtain a license or permit for that state. Other states will usually allow out-of-state hunters to purchase licenses in their state, but they sometimes charge a higher fee for nonresident hunters.

• Hunter safety requirement: most states require hunters to take and pass a hunter safety course, and have proof of that, before obtaining a license or permit.

Licensing and permit requirements and procedures vary by state. Contact your state's department of natural resources office or Web site to find out the specific rules for your state.

The Reason for the Season

Although some hunters dislike it, the closed season is a necessary element of hunting. The closed season allows proper wildlife management and ensures that animal populations will remain high enough to make hunting possible.

For most hunting seasons, the main reason for closed season is reproduction. During peak reproduction times, game must be left to mate and reproduce in order to maintain the population. Without this regulation, populations would dwindle. This would make hunting difficult to impossible and could even put animals in danger of extinction, at least in certain areas.

Another reason for the closed season, particular to game birds and waterfowl, is molting. At certain times during the year, birds molt, or shed worn and damaged feathers. New feathers grow in at the same time to replace these old feathers. Sometimes this can impair a bird's flying ability, which gives hunters an unfair advantage.

For hunters, it's important to always be mindful of hunting seasons and to follow these rules. Hunting seasons make it possible for the sport to continue safely and fairly.

Once a hunter gets a license or permit, it's important that he or she learn the proper rules and regulations of hunting, especially for the type of hunting being done. These rules and regulations vary from one type to another, depending on the animal being hunted and the area where the hunting takes place.

One of the major regulations to follow when hunting is being mindful of legal hunting seasons. Hunting seasons are specific times of the year when hunters are allowed to hunt certain animals. These

When hunting, wing shooters must be careful to hunt only in designated areas. Hunting on private property is illegal and considered trespassing.

dates vary by state and sometimes by region within the state. Hunting seasons help control the game population and must be observed by hunters. Hunting outside the season is illegal. Hunters can find out the specific dates for hunting seasons by contacting their state department of natural resources.

Another major rule is to hunt only in areas where hunting is permitted. Trespassing on private property to hunt or hunting in a preserve or animal sanctuary not designated as a legal hunting area is illegal. Hunters can be arrested for trespassing on private property or for hunting in protected areas.

Not only that, trespassing can be dangerous. In designated hunting areas, hunters are aware that there are others out hunting also. They know to be mindful of other hunters. But in an area not designated for hunting, there's no guarantee that other people on the property will know you're there. This makes it a very dangerous situation, one in which someone could accidentally get hurt or even killed because they're in the wrong place at the wrong time.

Identification is another important thing to be mindful of when hunting, especially with birds. Because it's often hard to distinguish protected or illegal species from legal species simply by sight, it's necessary to use other means of identification. Wing shooters must know flight patterns and characteristics, birdcalls, and habits to prevent shooting the wrong species by accident.

Hunters should also be aware of bag limits. These are limits on the number of animals a hunter may harvest and keep. In most cases, bag limits are imposed to prevent hunters from harvesting too many of a certain species, which could threaten the population size. Hunters who ignore or break these rules are called poachers.

Above all, it's critical to have consideration for fellow shooters. Make sure that you're aware of where they are, and they of you. Don't move around a lot, and try to avoid ruining their flight line. If you must pick up a bird, do so quickly, and get out of the way as soon as possible.

When wing shooting, there are many things to think about. It's important to take your time, be prepared, and make certain you follow all the necessary rules and regulations. Be sure to get the proper hunting safety training and have all the necessary licenses and permits. Know your gun, and how to properly handle it, and be careful to only hunt in designated areas. Always be mindful of your fellow hunters, and be very careful to know where they are, as well as make your own presence known to them. This is the only way you can have a safe, legal, and enjoyable time wing shooting.

CHAPTER 3

PLANNING THE HUNT

Like any activity, it's important to plan a hunting trip before you go. When using firearms, planning is essential. And with so many regulations and safety rules that hunters must follow, it's important to have a good idea of where to go, what is needed, and what you'll do when going on a hunting trip.

Hunting Preplanning

Before planning a wing-shooting trip, it's important to do a little pretrip preparation. The first step is to figure out where and when you're going to hunt. Being aware of hunting seasons is the next step. Hunters must know when hunting seasons begin and end so that they can plan their trip during the legal hunting season. Once a hunter knows when the season is open, he or she can plan the dates for the trip.

Another important thing to consider before planning a hunting trip is physical condition. Many people may not think about their physical condition before going hunting, but it's very important to avoid injury. Especially in wing shooting, hunters often have to do a great deal of walking to reach hunting spots or gather harvested game. It's important to be in good shape so that walking long distances won't be a problem. In addition to walking, wing shooters must have good upper body strength to control their guns or operate a bow. If hunters don't have enough body strength to properly handle a gun or bow, they run the risk of hurting themselves or others.

Shooting skeet or clays is a good way for wing shooters to practice before a hunt. The skeet or clays are small and shot into the air to simulate the quick movements of small birds.

In addition to strength and fatigue issues, hunters should always make sure they're healthy enough to hunt. If a hunter is sick and taking medicine, those medications could impair judgment and make hunting dangerous. And if a hunter is ill, spending long hours outdoors and exerting energy to walk and use weapons can make him or her even more ill. It's important to be healthy and in relatively good physical shape before going on a hunt.

Another important preparation for wing shooting is gaining a familiarity with bird behavior and habitats. This is essential for a number of reasons. First, it helps hunters find and identify game. Second, it helps hunters distinguish the birds they're trying to hunt from those they are not.

Before a wing-shooting hunt, many hunters like to get a little practice firing their guns and working on their aim. A good way to practice for a wing-shooting hunt is shooting skeet or clays. This is usually done on a shooting range. Clay discs are shot into the air by a machine, and hunters shoot at the discs. The discs fly through the air at high speeds, mimicking the speed of flying birds. Shooting skeet or clays can help hunters improve their aim and skill in shooting moving objects in the air.

Where to Hunt

Once you know the types of bird habitats, you must find the areas where these habitats are common. There are many resources out there for finding hunting areas for particular types of birds. After you decide which states or provinces are best for hunting a particular kind of bird, you can then search local resources to find legal hunting areas.

In general, these are the states and provinces where wing-shooting birds make their habitats:

- Doves: doves are most commonly found in open grassland and agricultural areas. Most U.S. states allow dove hunting. Doves aren't as prevalent in Canada, but they can be found and hunted in British Columbia and Quebec.
- Pheasants: pheasants thrive in a variety of land types. Grasslands, cropland, wetlands, and brush all provide habitats

Pheasants are commonly found in Midwestern states such as Kansas and Nebraska, and in Canadian provinces such as Ontario, Alberta, and Saskatchewan. Many hunters use dogs to help them retrieve harvested birds.

for pheasants. Iowa, Kansas, Minnesota, Nebraska, North Dakota, and South Dakota are some of the best states for hunting pheasants. Ontario, Alberta, and Saskatchewan offer good pheasant hunting opportunities in Canada.

- Grouse: grouse live primarily in young aspen forests and brushland. When aspen isn't available, oak, lowland brush,

Pheasants are one of the most commonly hunted birds. Male pheasants can have brightly colored feathers, which make them easier for hunters to spot.

and dense stands of trees are optional habitats. Michigan, Wisconsin, and Minnesota offer good opportunities for grouse hunting. Most of the Canadian provinces offer grouse hunting, as well.

- Chukars: chukars flock to arid, mountainous, and rocky areas. They can be found in many western states. Oregon, Idaho, Nevada, and Washington all have plenty of good chukar habitat areas. British Columbia offers chukar hunting in Canada.

Prehunt Checklist

Before going on a hunt, it's a good idea to make a checklist to be certain you have everything you'll need. Here are some items to include on that list:

1. License/permit. Be sure to have the proper license or permit in order to hunt legally.
2. Proper gun and ammunition. Be sure to have the right gun for the type of hunting you'll do, and be certain to have enough ammunition for the gun.
3. Hunting gear. Always have the appropriate gear for a hunt—plenty of hunter orange (vest, jacket, etc.), comfortable shoes, shooting glasses, and a coat.
4. Posthunt gear. In the event of harvesting game, it's important to have a sharp hunting knife, plastic bags, clean cloths or paper towels, and a cooler filled with ice for dressing and transporting harvested game.
5. Extra gear. Be sure to have plenty of food, water, sunscreen, maps, and anything else you'll need to be safe and comfortable on a hunt.

- Prairie chickens: as their name implies, prairie chickens are mostly found living in prairie grassland in states such as Nebraska, Missouri, Kansas, and Oklahoma. They usually prefer undisturbed tallgrass prairie, but they can also be found in agricultural and prairie mixed land. Prairie chicken hunting is not as big in Canada as it is in the United States, but it does occur in Alberta and Saskatchewan.

Once hunters decide which states or provinces are best for the type of bird they want to hunt, the next step is locating legal hunting areas. One good resource for locating proper hunting areas is the state department of natural resources or state wildlife management agencies. These departments usually regulate hunting areas within a state and help enforce state hunting laws.

Public hunting areas are maintained by the government of the state where they are located. Hunters can find information about these areas from their state department of natural resources. Usually, the state provides pamphlets and Web sites offering information about public hunting areas. Information about public hunting areas and hunting regulations can be obtained where licenses are sold. Hunting in these areas is often free or relatively inexpensive. That means they are very popular, which makes hunting on them a little more difficult because they can be crowded. But hunters can often obtain maps to research the hunting area and possibly find lesser-known spots.

Another good way to find hunting areas is to contact local sportsmen's clubs. These clubs often own private hunting land that they allow nonmembers to hunt on for a fee. They also know the area and its hunting lands better than anyone, so they can advise hunters on which places to go to legally hunt. There are also a number of Web sites and hunting organizations that maintain hunting area databases online.

When hunting, it is extremely important to always hunt on open land or in designated hunting areas. Wing shooters should never hunt on private or protected land because it's illegal to trespass and it can be dangerous.

With a little Internet research, most hunters can easily find a good place for hunting.

The main thing to remember when choosing a location for a hunt is to be certain it's specified as an open hunting area. Hunters should never trespass on private land or hunt in protected wildlife areas. Not only is this illegal and unethical, but it can also be dangerous.

When choosing a hunting area or preserve, there are several important things to consider:

- Amenities. Find out what kind of facilities the preserve offers—practice shooting areas, skeet ranges, food, and lodging are all good amenities to look for.
- Dog policy. Ask about a preserve's dog policy. If hunters are allowed to bring their own dogs, find out if there are kennels in the event of an overnight stay. If the preserve provides dogs and guides, find out what kind of dogs they use.
- Hunting style. Find out how you'll be hunting, be it on foot following a guide, from a four-wheel drive vehicle where you get out when the dogs go on point, or even, in some regions, traditional mule-drawn wagons. Also, if fitness or agility is a concern, ask how much walking will be involved and check how rugged the terrain will be.
- Ammunition. Some preserves include extra ammunition in their fees. Ask if that's the case before leaving to hunt.
- Paperwork. Certain states require different kinds of licenses and paperwork for hunting. Make sure the preserve can help you get the proper paperwork necessary to hunt in that state.
- Other hunters. A standard preserve hunt includes two hunters with a guide. Find out if that's the case before going on a hunt—some preserves allow more than two hunters to hunt at the same time.

Hunters should be sure to wear hunter orange, either on a hat, vest, or other piece of clothing. Wearing this bright color ensures that other hunters will be able to see you, helping to prevent accidents.

Preparing for the Hunt

When planning a hunting trip, of course things such as guns and ammunition come to mind as necessary items. But there are many other items hunters will need while on a hunting trip.

One of the most important things to get for a hunting trip is the proper clothing. With wing shooting, hunters often do a lot of walking, sometimes over rough terrain. Because of this, it's critical to get a comfortable pair of shoes that offers plenty of support and traction. Finding shoes or boots that are waterproof is even better, as feet need protection from the elements while on a hunt.

Another important piece of gear for bird hunters is a vest. A vest provides the perfect place to store shotgun shells, a bottle of water, other gear, and a camera. Most good bird-hunting vests are orange to help hunters stand out to other hunters (except with dove hunting, which is a sit-and-wait hunt, where it's important for the hunter to blend in with his or her surroundings). And good vests also have lots of pockets.

Many wing shooters also like to wear a hat with a brim while hunting. This shields the eyes from the sun and helps hunters see better. Sturdy shooting glasses are another must-have for wing-shooting trips. The best glasses protect the eyes by wrapping around the face, without blocking a hunter's view. Ear protection is also important while hunting. Guns are very loud, particularly because they're so close to the body when shooting. Electronic earmuffs protect the ears from loud sounds and also help hunters hear and locate their dogs.

A comfortable coat, particularly one that is waterproof, is also a good piece of gear to own. If it's cold out or it rains, hunters need a good coat to keep them warm and dry. Along with a coat, wing shooters also sometimes like to bring soft leather gloves on a hunt. These protect the hands from the elements and also help hunters hold their gun.

Another clothing item to consider for a wing-shooting trip is brush pants or chaps to protect the legs. These pants are specially made with rugged, tightly woven cotton to make them sturdy and to protect legs from briars, twigs, and other prickly brush. Brush pants and chaps are often made with a nylon layer or blend to give them additional sturdiness and provide further protection from scratches. Some pants also include a Teflon outer layer to make them waterproof.

Other items hunters might bring on a wing-shooting hunt include binoculars, a pair of hunting shears, and if they have a dog, an orange vest for their dog. Maps of the hunting area or a GPS unit are also helpful to avoid getting lost while hunting in unfamiliar areas. Sunscreen is good to bring on a hunt to protect skin against sunburn. And if a hunter will be out for a long time, it's also important to bring plenty of food and water to get through the day. Staying hydrated and fed will ensure the hunter stays healthy and able to hunt for as long as he or she pleases. But no matter what a hunter brings, he or she needs to be certain that clothing and gear are lightweight. A wing-shooting hunter is likely to do a lot of walking, so it's important to have clothing and items that are easily portable and won't weigh the hunter down or unnecessarily fatigue him or her.

CHAPTER 4

HUNTING

One of the most important choices a wing shooter can make in preparation for a hunt is selecting the correct gun. The correct gun can make all the difference between a successful and unsuccessful hunt.

For most wing-shooting purposes, a shotgun is the best firearm for a hunt. The ideal shotgun for a wing-shooting trip weighs around 7 pounds (3 kg). Lengthwise, the shotgun shouldn't be more than 4 feet long (1.2 meters).

Choosing a gauge is also important. For wing shooting, the ideal gauge is 16. But these can often be hard to find, so a 20-gauge shotgun serves as a good alternative to a 16-gauge. The 20-gauge shotgun can handle pretty much any wing-shooting fowl, and it has the capacity to hit small, fast-moving birds from a distance.

Wing shooting is best done with a gun that shoots rounds very quickly. Reloading

It's important for hunters to choose the right kind of gun for wing shooting. The most popular gun for this sport is the shotgun. Ideal gauges for wing shooting are 16- and 20-gauge.

takes up valuable time and can cause a hunter to miss opportunities. But, it's important to remember that when shooting migratory birds, such as doves, it is illegal to have a gun that shoots more than three shells at a time.

Hunting Technique

Once a hunter chooses his or her gun, the next important things to think about are hunting position and technique. When hunting

Quail hunters often use dogs to help them on a hunt. On a quail hunt, dogs move at a slow-to-moderate pace in order to find birds in small pockets of brush.

different kinds of birds, hunters must use different positioning and technique.

Quail

Hunting quail has gotten a lot more difficult for hunters due to modern land use practices. The clearing of brushland in many states has made it difficult for quail to find habitats. This makes it difficult for hunters to find good quail-hunting areas. Modern-day quail hunters must work harder to find quail "pockets," which are areas of brush cover where quail live.

Quail pockets can be very small sometimes, but a good hunter and his dog will check even the small spots, as these could yield good hunting. When hunting quail, hunters generally need only one dog, and the dog should move at a slow-to-moderate pace. When hunting these pockets, hunters should be careful not to overhunt one space. Harvesting one or two birds and then moving on to the next spot is the proper technique for responsible, ethical hunting.

Doves

Concealment is the name of the game for dove hunting. Because these birds use their keen sense of vision to spot predators, dove hunters must try to blend in with their surroundings. Wearing camouflage is common practice in dove hunting. Adding camouflage tape or finish to your gun will help disguise it from doves. Also, some hunters use camouflage greasepaint to minimize the shine on their faces.

Dove hunters scout potential hunting areas, usually with binoculars. Hunters should scout before 9 AM or after 3 PM, when birds are more likely to be moving. Some good places to find doves are fields of just-harvested grain crops, near bodies of water with wide areas of open mud along the shore, and gravelly sites such as rural roads, sandbars, and quarries.

Once a dove hunter finds a good location, he or she must stay put and try to blend into his or her surroundings as well as possible. A dove hunter must remain motionless until a dove gets within range, usually 25 to 35 yards (23 to 32 m). If a hunter moves too much or stands out too much from the surroundings, he or she can frighten the birds away.

Grouse

A dog is a hunter's best asset while grouse hunting. An important thing to remember when grouse hunting with dogs is to hunt into the wind. This allows the dog to pick up scents more easily.

Grouse generally live in brushy areas, where there's a nearby food source. It's sometimes difficult to figure out where grouse will be, so experienced grouse hunters often keep a log of their hunts. This allows them to see patterns and predict where they'll be most likely to find the birds.

Prairie Chickens

Prairie chicken hunters must search the tallgrass prairie meadows bordering agricultural land to find their game. Dogs can help hunters sniff out the prairie chicken.

Prairie chickens are fairly predictable in their behavioral patterns, making it easy to hunt them if a hunter is willing to take the time to observe and note the patterns. For instance, they often visit the same fields and feeding areas, usually around the same time of day. An observant hunter can note this and be ready when the prairie chicken makes a move.

Chukars

Chukars are a challenging bird for wing shooters to hunt. They often make their home in rough terrain, making it physically challenging to access the areas where they live. Chukars often live in rough, hilly areas. Although it may be the most painful option, climbing to the top of the hill may be the best plan for finding game. Chukars tend to stay at higher elevations to offer easier escape from predators.

When hunting chukars, it's best to hunt with a dog and stay in motion. Chukars move quickly, so when a dog spots one, the hunter needs to be at the ready in order to harvest the bird.

Once a hunter shoots a target, the next step is locating the animal and bagging it. But sometimes, that's easier said than done. Birds naturally blend into their surroundings, so when they fall back into the brush, it can almost seem as if they've disappeared. Having a dog on the hunt certainly helps, but there are some other techniques hunters can use to make sure they find and collect all harvested birds.

- When a hunter gets a good shot, it's natural to want to rush over and collect the bird. But hunters must fight that instinct

Chukars are challenging birds to hunt for two reasons. They often live in rough, hilly areas that may be difficult for a hunter to navigate, and they move very quickly.

and take a moment to stay put and observe their surroundings. This is important because no matter how obvious the fallen bird's position may seem, it may not be in the exact location a hunter thinks. But taking a moment to mark his or her position will help a hunter pinpoint where to base the search from and will allow him or her to return to that spot to wait for the next bird. But hunters shouldn't waste a lot of time marking position. It's very important to get to the bird quickly in case it wasn't fatally hit. A hunter doesn't want to leave a bird to suffer or escape and die later, which would be wasteful.

• A good signal to help hunters find downed birds is feathers floating in the air above the spot where the bird fell. A puff of feathers generally signals a solid hit. But hunters must be aware of wind when looking for feathers—the wind can move the feathers away from where the bird actually fell.

• Listening is another good technique for locating a downed bird. Chances are, the bird will still be moving after it has been shot, even if it's a clean shot. So hunters should listen for movement in the brush to locate their target. Hunters should not shoot birds on the ground.

- When searching for a downed bird, hunters should widen the search in tight circles beyond the spot where they think the bird fell.
- Hunters should also check tree and bush branches if they cannot find their quarry on the ground. It may have gotten tangled in the limbs or leaves of a tree or bush as it fell to the ground.
- Hunters should mark their shooting spot to allow them to walk the shot line where they were standing and where the bird may have fallen. Trail tape is good for marking the shot area, as is throwing down your hunting cap.

Group Hunting

While many wing shooters prefer to hunt alone or with maybe one other person, group hunts are common in wing shooting. Especially on preserves, larger groups of hunters, often led by a guide and his or her dogs, are the common form of wing-shooting hunts.

Many of the same rules apply to individual hunts and group hunts. But group hunts present a special set of rules and etiquette to follow. Before going on the trip, hunters should check with the rest of the group to be certain there's not a dress code. Some groups require hunters to wear a certain amount of hunter orange or certain types of gear. If there is a dress code within the group, it's important for all hunters to follow it.

Dogs are also important on group hunts. Before going on the trip, the entire group should be aware who's bringing dogs and how many there will be. Hunters should all be aware of the dogs and be prepared to hunt with them.

Dogs on the Hunt

Dogs are great to have while wing shooting. Generally, wing shooters choose pointers and spaniels as their hunting dogs. These dogs rely on their sense of smell to find and point out game birds. Spaniels and pointers share many traits that make them ideal for wing shooting—powerful sense of smell, stamina, intelligence, affinity for water, speed, and courage. Additionally, these dogs are generally outgoing, well-mannered, and friendly, making them perfect for hunts.

At ground level, dogs detect things humans typically miss. In high grass, cornfields, and woods, it's best to let the dog follow its nose. Once it finds a scent and points out a spot, the hunter can move forward.

When hunting on a preserve with a guide and his or her dogs, it's best for hunters to avoid interfering with the handler and the dogs. These dogs are used to working with their handler and can respond to hand signals, whistles, and voice commands that only the handler and dog know. These dogs are trained to obey only their handlers, so attempting to command them is pointless and detrimental to the hunt. Even if a hunter wants to just pet the dog, he or she should always ask the handler first.

When hunting with dogs, it's important to be aware and careful not to shoot below eye level. Just as hunters must look out for themselves and other hunters, they must be careful for the safety of their dogs.

Safety when hunting with a group is extremely important. Because there are more people, and sometimes more dogs, it's critical for hunters to be aware of fellow hunters and their dogs at all times. These tips will help keep wing shooters safe in a group hunt setting:

Dogs are a great asset to wing shooters during a hunt. They use their strong sense of smell and keen hearing to help hunters locate and retrieve birds.

- Stay in line with other hunters. Do not get ahead or behind other hunters.
- When swinging through a shot, do not point or fire the gun in the vicinity of fellow shooters. Always be aware of your surroundings.
- Be careful of dogs when shooting. Do not rush the shot or shoot below eye level.
- If your gun is an autoloader, be sure to use a guard to prevent ejecting shells from hitting fellow hunters or their equipment.

In addition to safety considerations, hunters must follow special etiquette when participating in a group hunt. When choosing shots, hunters shouldn't go for a bird that might make a better target for another hunter. It's important to choose shots carefully. And along those same lines, hunters should strive for clean shots each time. Not only is this helpful to other hunters, it's the humane and ethical way to hunt.

Another thing to keep in mind is general behavior on a group hunt. Excessive talking or loudness is rude and detrimental to other hunters. And staying together is another key rule to remember when hunting with a group. If one member wanders off and becomes separated from the group, they can waste valuable hunting time trying to find him or her. In addition, it's dangerous to wander off from the group because it's easy to get lost or hurt.

CHAPTER 5

AFTER THE HUNT

When a successful hunt ends, the next step for hunters is transporting and dressing the harvested game. These steps are critical in order to maintain the harvested game for eating. This part of the hunt is also important because hunters will likely use knives, and they must be especially careful to prevent injury.

Handling Harvested Fowl

As a hunter begins to transport and dress the harvested game, certain tools will be necessary. A sharp hunting knife, resealable plastic bags, clean cloths or paper towels, and a cooler full of ice are essential. While still in the field, it's advisable to begin the process of dressing—preparing the game for eating—immediately. The first step is to remove the entrails—stomach, intestines, etc. If there is food inside the bird, specifically grain or corn, it must be removed.

Hunters should bring a sharp hunting knife along in order to dress harvested birds. To ensure freshness of the meat, hunters must often begin the dressing process in the field.

Otherwise, the grain can ferment and ruin the meat. The heart and liver of many game birds can be used for giblets, which are the edible internal organs of a bird, often used in gravies. These must be stored in a plastic bag and kept clean and cold. Once the interior cavity of the bird has been cleared of entrails, wipe it down with a clean cloth.

Some states require hunters to make an identifying mark on birds to verify they are legal harvests. Birds may be plucked and skinned in the field. If the bird is plucked or skinned in the field, it's important to save the feathers in a plastic bag for identification purposes.

Quail can be cooked many different ways, such as wrapped in bacon. To properly cook harvested birds, the hunter must first determine the age of the bird.

It's very important to cool harvested game quickly. The birds should be placed in plastic bags and put on ice. This keeps the meat from being contaminated by bacteria, and it also helps the meat retain its flavor. Birds should not be piled on top of each other—there should be a little ice between each so that they cool properly. When putting the cooler into the car, it should be stored in the car's cabin and not in the trunk. The trunk's enclosed space does not allow the heat to escape the birds as easily. And because of this, it's also important to keep the car cabin well ventilated.

Once the birds are back home, they must be dressed. Hunters should wash hands, knives, and cutting boards or surfaces thoroughly with hot, soapy water before preparing the harvested game. If the bird hasn't already been plucked and skinned, it should be done at this time. Once the bird has been plucked and skinned, it should be soaked in cold water, often with salt added, for an hour or so to help remove excess blood.

Once the excess blood is removed, hunters use knives to cut the game into usable pieces—breasts, drumsticks, etc. If the meat will be eaten soon, it can be stored in the refrigerator. If it won't be eaten in the next couple of days, the meat should be frozen to retain freshness and flavor. The meat should be wrapped tightly in freezer wrap or aluminum foil, and then placed inside plastic freezer bags or stored on a freezer bag filled with water. Wrapping tightly is necessary to remove excess air from the package. It's important to label the meat with a date, as it should be used within a year of the hunt.

When preparing harvested game for eating, the age of the bird dictates how to cook it. Different cooking methods apply for birds of different ages. A hunter can determine the bird's age by checking the beak, breastbones, and legs. Younger birds have flexible beaks, softer breastbones, and lighter legs. Older birds have inflexible beaks, brittle breastbones, and darker, hard-skinned legs. For younger birds, dry cooking methods such as frying work best. For older birds, moist cooking methods such as stewing or braising are the way to go.

Taxidermy

While some people use the game they harvest for food, others choose to preserve their birds with taxidermy. Taxidermy is the practice of stuffing and mounting dead animals for display. Many people do this to preserve the birds they harvest, often displaying them in their homes and sometimes even in museums. Taxidermy is a fairly popular hobby in the United States and Canada.

The goal in taxidermy is to make the animal look as lifelike as possible. Harvested animals are generally frozen whole until the taxidermist is ready to prepare them. He or she then skins the bird and treats the skin with chemicals to keep it from decomposing. Then the taxidermist measures and poses the remaining muscle fibers and bones. The taxidermist uses those measurements to make a plaster mold. The mold is used to create the internal base of the body, and the treated skin and feathers are then placed over the internal base. Taxidermists sometimes use glass eyes and artificial teeth for mammals.

One of the keys to making the bird look lifelike is posing. Many birds are posed to look as though they're in flight, displaying their wings. If a bird doesn't fly in nature, it's best to pose it in a standing position. Regardless of how they are posed, birds preserved through taxidermy allow hunters to enjoy their hunt for years to come.

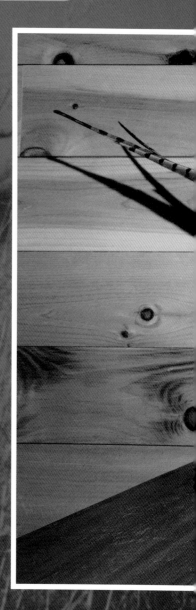

Taxidermy is a popular hobby and a good way to preserve harvested birds. Many hunters use preserved birds as decorations in their homes.

Many people say they don't like to eat wild birds because of the "wild" or "gamey" taste. A good way to minimize this is to be certain to trim off as much of the fat as possible. Another good method for reducing the strong flavor, and helping the meat maintain moisture, is to wrap it in bacon. When cooking harvested game, the most important thing to remember is to make sure the meat is thoroughly cooked. The internal temperature of the meat should be at least 165 degrees Fahrenheit (74 degrees Celsius). For accuracy, you can use a meat thermometer to check the meat to make sure it's done. The juices should run clear, and no pinkness should remain in the meat.

caliber The approximate diameter of the barrel, and by extension, the projectile used in it, measured in inches or millimeters.

cartridge Also called a round, a cartridge packages the bullet, gunpowder, and primer into a single metallic case made to fit the firing chamber of a gun.

chukar A grayish-brown Eurasian partridge; an upland bird in the pheasant family.

cover A brushy or grassy area used by birds for shelter and hiding.

dove A small, wild pigeon.

dressing Skinning, plucking, cutting up, and preparing a bird/animal for eating.

entrails Internal organs including the stomach and intestines.

fowl Another name for birds.

game Wild animals hunted for food and sport.

gauge The size of a shotgun barrel's inner diameter numerically measured by the number of lead balls it can contain.

giblets Edible internal organs of birds, including the heart, liver, and gizzard.

grouse Small, reddish-brown ground-dwelling bird.

habitat The environment where an animal normally lives.

hunter orange A bright orange hue used on clothing for hunters. The bright color allows hunters to be seen in wooded or brush areas.

pheasant Large, long-tailed wild bird.

pointer A breed of dog popular for use with hunters.

prairie A treeless, grassy plain area.

prairie chicken Large, henlike grouse bird that lives in North American prairie lands.

preserve An area where hunting is permitted during certain months.

round See cartridge.

shell A self-contained cartridge or bullet used in shotguns.

shotgun A firearm used in hunting that is usually designed to fire from the shoulder.

skeet The sport of shooting at clay disks that are hurled upward in such a way as to simulate the flight of a bird.

taxidermy The act of preserving and mounting dead animals for display.

trespassing Entering private property without permission.

upland hunting An American term for a form of bird hunting in which the hunter pursues upland birds including quail, pheasant, grouse, chukar, and prairie chicken.

wing shooting Shooting game birds that are in flight.

Canadian Wildlife Service

Environment Canada

Ottawa, ON K1A 0H3

Canada

(819) 997-2800

Web site: http://www.cws-scf.ec.gc.ca

The Canadian Wildlife Service handles wildlife matters that are the responsibility of the federal government.

International Hunter Education Association (IHEA)

2727 W. 92nd Avenue, Suite 103

Federal Heights, CO 80260

(303) 430-7233

Web site: http://www.ihea.com

The IHEA is the professional association for sixty-seven state and provincial wildlife conservation agencies and the seventy thousand volunteer instructors who teach hunter education in North America.

Natural Resources Canada

580 Booth Street

Ottawa, ON K1A 0E4

Canada

(613) 995-0947

Web site: http://www.nrcan-rncan.gc.ca

Natural Resources Canada champions innovation and expertise in earth sciences, forestry, energy, and minerals and metals to ensure the responsible and sustainable development of Canada's natural resources.

U.S. Fish and Wildlife Service

4401 N. Fairfax Drive, Suite 340

Arlington, VA 22203

Web site: http://www.fws.gov

The mission of the U.S. Fish and Wildlife Service is to work with others to conserve, protect, and enhance fish, wildlife, plants, and their habitats for the continuing benefit of the American people.

U.S. Natural Resources Conservation Service (NRCS)

P.O. Box 2890

Washington, DC 20013

Web site: http://www.nrcs.usda.gov

The NRCS works with landowners on conservation planning and assistance designed to benefit the soil, water, air, plants, and animals that result in productive lands and healthy ecosystems.

Web Sites

Due to the changing nature of Internet links, Rosen Publishing has developed an online list of Web sites related to the subject of this book. This site is updated regularly. Please use this link to access the list:

http://www.rosenlinks.com/hunt/wing

Boyer, Terry. *Hunter's Guide to Shotguns for Upland Game*. Mechanicsburg, PA: Stackpole Books, 2007.

Cassell, Jay. *The Gigantic Book of Hunting Stories*. New York, NY: Skyhorse Publishing, 2008.

The Complete Book of Upland Bird Hunting: Essentials for Success in Field, Farm & Forest. New York, NY: Shady Oak Press, 2007.

Grooms, Steve. *Modern Pheasant Hunting*. Mechanicsburg, PA: Stackpole Books, 2005.

Otto, John R. *A Season of Wing Shooting*. Bloomington, IN: Xlibris Corporation, 2007.

Tapply, William G. *Upland Autumn: Birds, Dogs, and Shotgun Shells*. New York, NY: Skyhorse Publishing, 2009.

Underwood, Lamar. *1001 Hunting Tips: The Ultimate Guide—Deer, Upland Game and Birds, Waterfowl, Big Game*. New York, NY: Skyhorse Publishing, 2010.

BIBLIOGRAPHY

Ayres, James Morgan, and Rick Sapp. *The Complete Gun Owner: Your Guide to Selection, Use, Safety and Laws*. Iola, WI: Krause Publications, 2008.

Bowlen, Bruce. *The Orvis Wingshooting Handbook, Fully Revised and Updated: Proven Techniques for Better Shotgunning*. Guilford, CT: The Lyon's Press, 2008.

Boyer, Terry. *Hunter's Guide to Shotguns for Upland Game*. Mechanicsburg, PA: Stackpole Books, 2007.

Brant, Alex. *The Complete Guide to Wing Shooting: The Ultimate Handbook to a Specialized Sport*. Guilford, CT: The Lyon's Press, 2005.

Casada, Jim. "Getting Started (or Re-started) in Bird Hunting." Wingshooting USA. Retrieved February 8, 2010 (http://www.wingshootingusa.org/Bird_Hunting_Library/Getting_Started.cfm).

Deck, Tom. *The Orvis Guide to Gunfitting: Techniques to Improve Your Wingshooting, and the Fundamentals of Gunfit*. Guilford, CT: The Lyons Press, 2006.

Eagle, Karen. *The Everything Wild Game Cookbook: From Fowl and Fish to Rabbit and Venison—300 Recipes for Home-Cooked Meals* (Everything: Cooking). Avon, MA: Adams Media, 2006.

Faw, Michael D. "Geared for a Day Afield." Wingshooting USA. Retrieved February 8, 2010 (http://www.wingshootingusa.org/Bird_Hunting_Library/geared.cfm).

Garden-Robinson, Julie. "From Field to Table…A Pocket Guide to Care and Handling of Game Birds." Retrieved February 8, 2010 (http://www.ag.ndsu.edu/pubs/yf/foods/ncr527w.htm).

Grooms, Steve. *Modern Pheasant Hunting*. Mechanicsburg, PA: Stackpole Books, 2005.

International Hunter Education Association. "Hunter Safety Requirements." Retrieved February 8, 2010 (http://www.ihea.com/hunter-education/hunter-education requirements.php).

Lewis, Gary. *Complete Guide to Hunting: Basic Techniques for Gun & Bow Hunters* (The Complete Hunter). Minneapolis, MN: Creative Publishing international, 2008.

Lyons, Larry. *The Gun Owner's Handbook: A Complete Guide to Maintaining and Repairing Your Firearms—in the Field or at Your Workbench*. Guilford, CT: The Lyons Press, 2006.

Triplett, Todd. *The Complete Guide to Upland Bird Taxidermy: How to Prepare and Preserve Pheasants, Grouse, Quail, and Other Gamebirds*. Guilford, CT: Globe Pequot Press, 2006.

Williams, Ben O. *Wingshooting Wisdom: Prairie: A Guidebook for Finding & Hunting Public Lands*. Minocqua, WI: Willow Creek Press, 2006.

INDEX

A

age, determining a bird's, 51
ammunition, 10, 29, 32, 34
animal sanctuaries, 22
archery equipment, 4, 6, 10, 25

B

bag limits, 22
binoculars, 35, 40
birdcalls, 22
brush pants/chaps, 35

C

camouflage, 40
Canada, 4, 10, 27, 29, 30, 52
chukars, 6, 29, 41
clays, shooting, 26
closed seasons, 20
conservation laws, 4–5
cooking methods, 51, 54

D

deer, 4, 14
dogs, hunting, 4, 6, 32, 34, 35, 39, 40, 41,
     44, 45, 47
doves, 6, 27, 34, 37, 40
dress codes, 44
dressing process, 29, 48–49, 51

E

ear protection, 13, 34
entrails, 48, 49
etiquette, hunting, 44, 47
extinction, 20

G

game, identifying, 13, 15–16, 22, 26, 49
giblets, 49
glasses, hunting, 16, 29, 34
GPS units, 35
greasepaint, 40
group hunting, 44–45, 47
grouse, 6, 28–29, 40
gun safety, 6, 10, 12–13, 15, 23, 45, 47

H

harvested fowl, 4, 22, 25, 29, 39, 41,
     43–44, 48–49, 51, 52, 54
hunter orange, 14, 15, 29, 34, 35, 44
hunter safety practices, 6, 14, 15–16,
     22–23, 45, 47
hypothermia, 15

I

International Hunter Education
     Association (IHEA), 13, 16

L

licenses, hunting, 6, 13, 17, 19–20, 23, 29,
     30, 32

M

maps, 29, 30, 35
molting, 20

N

natural resources, departments of, 16,
     19, 22, 30

O

overhunting, 5
overpopulation, 4
over/under shotguns, 7

P

permits, hunting, 6, 17, 19–20, 23, 29
pheasants, 6, 27–28
poachers, 22
pointers, 45
prairie chickens, 6, 30, 41
prehunt checklist, 29
preserves, 22, 30, 44, 45

Q

quail, 39

R

rules and regulations, hunting, 6, 13, 15,
    17, 19–20, 22–23, 24, 30, 44–45, 47

S

safety courses, 6, 19
seasons, hunting, 5, 20, 22, 24

semiautomatic shotguns, 7
shotgun gauges, 9–10, 36
skeet shooting, 26, 32
spaniels, 45
sportsmen's clubs, 30

T

taxidermy, 52
technique, hunting, 32, 37, 39
trail tape, 44
trespassing, 22, 32

U

upland hunting, 6, 7
upland shotguns, 7

W

wildlife management agencies, 30
wing shooting
    after the hunt, 29, 48–54
    during the hunt, 36–47
    hunter education, 7–16
    hunter responsibility, 17–23
    overview, 4–7
    planning the hunt, 24–35

About the Author

Jennifer Bringle grew up in a family of hunters in North Carolina. She has written several other books for children and teens on a variety of subjects.

About the Consultant

Benjamin Cowan has more than twenty years of both big game and small game hunting experience. In addition to being an avid hunter, Cowan is also a member of many conservation organizations. He currently resides in west Tennessee.

Photo Credits

Cover, pp. 1, 3, 7, 14, 17, 24, 36, 48 David De Lossy/Photodisc/Thinkstock; back cover (silhouette) Hemera/Thinkstock; pp. 5. 8–9, 25, 27, 28, 31, 33, 37, 42–43, 49, 50 Shutterstock.com; pp. 7, 17, 24, 36, 48 (silhouette) © www.istockphoto.com/Michael Olson and Hemera/Thinkstock; pp. 10–11 Comstock/Thinkstock; pp. 12–13 © AP Images; pp. 18–19 U.S. Fish & Wildlife Service; pp. 20, 29, 45, 52–53 (background) Michael Melford/Stone/ Getty Images; p. 21 Lenora Gim/Photonica/Getty Images; pp. 38–39 John Rottet/MCT/Landov; p. 46 Charles Platiau/Reuters/Landov; pp. 52–53 Brian Kennedy/Workbook Stock/Getty Images; book art (camouflage) © www. istockphoto.com/Dar Yang Yan.

Designer: Nicole Russo, Editor: Bethany Bryan;
Photo Researcher: Marty Levick